MY HEALING FROM GAMBLING & ALCOHOL IN MEDJUGORJE

To, Moira
God bless & best wishes

First Published October 2004
Second Publication May 2007

Publisher:
Arthur McCluskey,
Borraderra, Monasterevin,
Co. Kildare, Ireland.

DEDICATION

This book is dedicated to my brother Eamonn. I also dedicate it in a very special way to my mother whose incredible prayer and faith, hopefully strengthened also by my new prayer life, will carry me forward to spread the message of a Mother's love and prayers that are so important to all our lives. Our Blessed Mother through her messages in Medjugorje constantly asks us to pray, pray, pray from the heart. She also says, "if you only knew how much I love you, you would cry tears of joy". Your Heavenly Mother is calling you to conversion. Are you alert and listening?

ACKNOWLEDGMENTS

I am most grateful to everyone who has helped with the production of this book, especially to my friends who did a lot of research and proof reading but wish to remain anonymous. God bless you all.

CONTENTS

PREFACE

Arthur McCluskey has been in the business world for many years and his self-reliance and independence has contributed to his unequivocal success. For almost thirty years Arthur had drifted from his faith and he seemed to have found a good life without it. He enjoyed the highlife of gambling and socialising. In the modern world he had made it. So it is amazing that Arthur's life has been completely changed.

In June 1999, Arthur reluctantly went to Medjugorje. A series of events took place that week that irreversibly changed his life. These events he shares with us in this testimony. It is the story of two mothers; the Mother in Heaven and his mother on Earth; the Rosary, with the melting of hearts, followed by conversion. Some of the events that took place seem very strange. However, the reader is not asked to accept or reject, but to understand that he shares these private revelations with us. The result is that Arthur is a very changed man. He no longer takes alcohol and has stopped gambling. His experiences suggest that we can be freed from whatever enslaves us through conversion to God.

Since his conversion Arthur has made many trips to Medjugorje. It was on one of these trips that my two sons met Arthur. They were aged thirteen and sixteen years at the time and they were duly impressed with a man who turned his back on his old life and had set his goal on following the path of Jesus Christ. Arthur's easy way with young people and his willingness to listen to their voices, served as a witness to my sons as the message of Our Lady of Medjugorje took on a new and relevant meaning, "I have come to invite you to your individual conversion."

Our Lady is presently coming to Medjugorje, calling us back to God. The wonderful love that Our Lady wants to bring us towards, is aptly expressed in the Holy Bible in Isaiah 49: 13-17:

> "Can a mother forget her infant, be without tenderness for the child of her womb, even should she forget, I will never forget you, see upon the palms of my hands, I have written your name."

Since Arthur's first journey to Medjugorje he has answered God's call and committed himself to God's Will. This has led him to set up a charitable organisation called "St. Joseph and The Helpers" in order to reach out and support other charitable organisations in Bosnia and Herzegovina. I have no doubt, that in reading his story, you too will hear your own special call from God.

Dr. Colm Smith
October, 2004.

FOREWORD

Reading the testimony of Mr Arthur McCluskey one goes from one surprise to the next. The drama of the money stolen from the family friend was a trigger to a new life and opened the Pandora box of the years to come. Competition with no mercy and the rude life trying to steal as much pleasure as possible out of one's own body and gain power over the people and things through immoral living and gambling was a desperate plea and search for happiness. Winning in the gambling always proved to him that he needed to go for it again and losing was a reason anyway to come again to regain the loss. People in the surroundings became a part of a large game of personal agenda where hardly anyone meant anything. There was only a hidden, almost totally suppressed, memory and respect for few family members, people like the mother who remained always like a spark of grace of God to keep open line to the return.

When we read the story of Arthur it is like reading a map to understand the paths of what is happening to the people living that style of life in business, affected by addiction and alcohol. Here one understands better why people behave like they do and why the world is becoming so threatening and with no mercy. Reading this story we understand better why Our Lord and Our Lady desire to reach out into the lives and the minds of contemporary mentality of humanity to bring the sacraments for those who became the prisoners in the chains that squeeze even harder than those in jails.

I recommend this testimony to people who want to understand better the business mixed with evil often happening even in our families and in our neighbourhoods. With this testimony we have more reason to pray for people involved in gambling, drinking and other common evil of our culture. I see Arthur as a witness of how God wants to bring graces to people who are in the most need of His mercy.

Father Svetozar Kraljevic, OFM, Medjugorje.
October, 2004.

The Cross on Cross-Mountain that became flesh in my hands

MEDJUGORJE

The twentieth century will take its place in the history of the universe as the most revolutionary and extraordinary of any of its predecessors, with mankind pushing the boundaries of civilisation far beyond the confines of Earth. The discovery of nuclear power; the breaking of the sound barrier; genetic engineering and man's first walk on the moon are to name a few achievements which have caught the imagination of the world; but in a little hamlet called Medjugorje[1] in Bosnia & Herzegovina, something extraordinary occurred that may overshadow all other events of the twentieth century.

On the 24th June 1981, on the Feast of St. John the Baptist, an event took place which transformed the lives of the peasant farmers who lived in Medjugorje and has since impacted on thousands of people throughout the world. It was preceded by a storm of such intensity and ferocity as has never been experienced there, before or since. During the calm after the storm on a rock strewn hillside above their homes, six children witnessed the appearance of a beautiful woman and child, the Blessed Virgin Mary and her Son Jesus and since that day, over twenty-three years ago, Mary has made a daily appearance to the young people she has chosen as her visionaries.

This sort of phenomenon did not cease at the close of the "Apostolic era,"[2] since then other phenomena have been reported and experienced throughout the world in places such as Knock in Ireland, Fatima in Portugal and Lourdes in France, just to mention a few. The appearances of Mary at these places have been accompanied by much controversy and Medjugorje is no exception in this respect, especially as it is purported that "secrets" of a prophetic nature have been imparted to the visionaries, as they were in Fatima. The Church has approved many of the phenomenal appearances of Mary but Medjugorje is still under investigation and this can only be completed when the visionaries announce that the apparitions have ceased.

1 The name translates "between the hills".

2 Since the time of Jesus.

The Late Holy Father, John Paul II, by virtue of his position as the Vicar of Christ in the Roman Catholic Church, kept under observation the events in Medjugorje. However, on returning from Poland to Rome in August 2002 he sent to Fr. Jozo, the parish priest of Medjugorje when the apparitions first occurred, his apostolic blessing and thanks for the great courtesy and kindness extended to pilgrims from the people in Bosnia & Herzegovina. As far as I am aware our present Pope Benedict XVI has not made any comments on the apparitions in Medjugorje, though it is alleged that he made two private visits when he was a Cardinal.

Jesus said, "I must be about my Father's business."[3] Our Lady has been entrusted with the solemn mission of fulfiling God's Will and bringing to a happy conclusion the work of her Son; the salvation of the entire world. This is a world where people are searching for guidance, direction and peace and where the Kingdom of God is struggling to survive. Her message, in short, is that this is now a defining moment for the world, for all of us.

Medjugorje is a place of peace, reminding us that materialistic things of the world do not bring us happiness. It is a place where people find time to talk to God and to each other. It is there for everyone, of all nationalities, of all ages, religions and creeds and for those who are seeking the truth about life. God came to find the one lost sheep.[4] He is searching for each and every one of us. Conversion causes a supernatural awakening in a person's life which brings that person to an awareness of God.

3 Luke 2: 49-50
4 Matthew 18: 12-14

INTRODUCTION

My name is Arthur McCluskey. I was brought up in the village of Emo, County Laois, Ireland where my father was the principal of the local school. I am the seventh of eight children, six sisters and an older brother. My parents were traditional Irish Catholics and we prayed the Rosary every evening. Church activities featured strongly in our daily lives, no television in those days! Growing up, I was very fond of Gaelic football, shooting, rugby and I played football for the under fourteen, minor and senior teams for County Laois. In 1964 I emigrated from Ireland to Scotland and lived in Glasgow for nearly thirty-six years.

In 1971 I set up my own mail order and furnishing business, which became very successful. Within a couple of years I owned a string of racehorses and over a period of time I had about thirty winners throughout Ireland and the UK. I flew regularly on Concorde and enjoyed first class travel on jumbo jets to exotic places throughout the world. There was no scarcity of money to fund my champagne lifestyle. However, in the midst of this grandiose and hedonistic way of life I was a compulsive racehorse gambler, often losing in excess of £30,000 a day.

Over the years my attitude to the Catholic and Protestant Churches cooled. I was cynical of the messages from the pulpit. I felt that I was exposed to nothing but hypocrisy in the religious world. The clergy preached the gospel of Christ from the pulpit but appeared to disregard the message in their own lives. My earlier upbringing to respect clergy had been eroded. I was an occasional churchgoer and had been to confession once in thirty years.

DEATH AND CONTRITION

My brother Eamonn came to work for my furnishing company in Glasgow early in 1981 after a career in hotel management and a failed marriage. Three years later he died suddenly from cancer. His friend had rushed him to hospital after ringing me urgently. My brother had been coughing up blood. The next day, at five o'clock in the evening, the surgeon informed me that Eamonn had, at most, six months to live. One lung and two vertebrae had already been eaten away by cancer and he gave him no hope of survival. I was shattered. At ten o'clock that evening I received an urgent phone call from the hospital to say Eamonn was dead. I very much regretted not seeing him before he died – especially since we had a falling out sometime beforehand. However, I thanked God for taking him as he did. It would have been extremely hard for Eamonn to endure a slow death and for my mother and family to witness his suffering.

I was at the hospital twenty minutes after the telephone message. I knelt down beside Eamonn and quietly prayed the act of contrition[5] into his ear. I continued praying and whilst praying the Hail Mary[6] I became aware of what sounded like a male voice speaking the prayer in my ear; I know the difference between a thought and actually hearing a voice. It was as if the words were spoken through an earphone, repeated very slowly, and amplified in my head so that by the end of three Hail Marys I felt for the first time in my life that I knew the meaning of the prayer. I was nearly forty years of age at that time.

Some months after Eamonn's funeral I met my cousin, a Catholic Priest, and I told him about my experience whilst praying the Hail Mary at Eamonn's deathbed. He said death always brought home to him the meaning of prayer and he could well understand what I experienced. Nothing more was said and I put the episode down to shock, as it looked like this happened to others when confronting a death.

5 "Contrition is a heartfelt sorrow for past sin accompanied by the intention not to sin again". (O'Collins and Farrugia, 2000, p.53) An "act of contrition" is a means, one of which is prayer, of obtaining forgiveness of sin: efforts at reconciliation with one's neighbour, tears of repentance, concern for the salvation of one's neighbour—" (CCC 1434).

6 A treasured prayer based on the angel Gabriel's greeting to Mary at the Annunciation and on Elizabeth's greeting when Mary visited her (CCC 2676; Bauer, J. 1999, p.212).

SLOW ROAD TO MEDJUGORJE

The Christmas after Eamonn's death a family member called Eleanor showed me a video she had taken during an apparent apparition in Medjugorje, Bosnia and Herzegovina.

I had never heard of the place beforehand and she explained some of the background. Our Lady[7] first appeared there in 1981. At that time the Communist party was the ruling party in the country. Their philosophy was atheism which is total denial of the existence of God and a belief in the supremacy of the state. When the people started to flock to Medjugorje in their hundreds and thousands, the communist leaders reacted by placing their guards throughout Medjugorje in order to discourage them from going to the site of the apparitions. This was done through non-verbal intimidation and harassment. Due to the disruptions created by the people and the communist guards, the sites of the apparitions had to be changed regularly, very often under direction from Our Lady to the visionaries.

We watched the video which showed the six young visionaries, Ivanka,Vicka, Ivan, Mirjana, Marija and Jakov praying the Rosary[8] in Croatian. There were other people in the room who were invited to attend the apparition. Everyone was praying at the same pace, when suddenly and in unison, all the visionaries dropped to their knees and looked up towards the ceiling where they were apparently seeing Our Lady. They immediately began to pray at a much slower pace than everyone else in the room. Afterwards I asked about this and was told that the visionaries were praying at the same pace as Our Lady. The pace of their prayer instantly took me back to my brother's deathbed and I commented that I would like to go to Medjugorje some day.

7 The title used for the Blessed Virgin Mary that is affectionately used most often by English Speaking Catholics (Bauer, J. 1999, p. 227).

8 Meaning a circle or crown of roses. These were originally beads in the shape of roses, in a circle. Praying each bead is a form of meditation and repetitive prayer. "In the Catholic Church this form of meditation has always focused on Mary, the mother of Christ and on her mysterious and beautiful relationship with her son, Jesus". (Groeschel, 1995, p.3).

About five years after I had seen the video, Eleanor gave me a string of white Rosary Beads from Medjugorje and I promptly consigned them to a dressing table drawer. I had no need for Rosary Beads with my lifestyle. I told a former girl friend about the beads and she said that a friend of hers in Dublin had Rosary Beads from Medjugorje, which had inexplicably changed colour.[9] "You had better keep an eye on them," she said with a mischievous smile. Over the years I have to admit to taking the odd peep, to see if the white beads had changed colour to blue, the other colour I associate with Our Lady from pictures and statues.

At a family wedding in February 1999 I was invited by Eleanor's husband Joe to go to Medjugorje the following June, either the first or second week. In the heat of the moment and in a very inebriated state, I agreed. The next day, in a more sober frame of mind, I thought very differently. I was looking for a way out, as I had no interest in going. On my return to Glasgow I remembered that I had the ideal reason for not going. I had already committed myself to a golfing trip in County Kerry with three Scottish friends, which straddled the first two weeks in June.

I could not wait to get hold of Joe on the telephone to impart my news. Our conversation went something like this: "Joe, Arthur here." "The very man," said Joe, "I was just about to telephone you! I got the dates wrong; Eleanor is not going until the 23rd of June!" Can you go then?" My diary for the 23rd and the following week were clear. I heard myself say, "Yes I could go then." "That's great," said Joe. The conversation ended and I am unable to consign to print the exact words I used in my own chastisement, except to say, the second word was perhaps something like "idiot"! Why didn't I tell him a lie? However, I felt I still had plenty of time for a sound business excuse to crop up for not going!

9 Phenomena of Medjugorje where plastic beads and cords change colour and silver coloured wire cords turn to a gold colour.

A short time later Eleanor told me Medjugorje was all about confession and conversion[10]. "That does not concern me," I responded, "I am only going for the beer!" I paid my deposit to Marian Pilgrimages in Dublin but secretly hoped the war in Kosovo, Yugoslavia would give me the desired excuse not to go but I was not let off the hook!

A week before departure I told a Presbyterian friend in Glasgow of my plans and how I was dreading the whole idea. "You never know, it could do you a lot of good," he said. He hadn't said what I wanted to hear, but as a real friend I knew he was speaking from the heart, genuinely believing the trip would do me good. I told another couple of friends and they gasped, "you above all people going on a pilgrimage; what is the world coming to?" The night before departure a thought prompted me to bring the Rosary Beads. The next morning, I was literally out the front door, when I was prompted a second time to run back into the house and retrieve them.

10 The call of God to all of us; to convert, to change our lives.

JOURNEY AND FIRST DAY

At Dublin Airport I was introduced to other members of the group and I established that some of them were regular visitors to other Marian Shrines. "What am I doing with a shower of professional pilgrimage holidaymakers?" I thought. "How will I stick this for seven days?" Eleanor, our group leader, gave me a leaflet to read on Medjugorje. I wished that she had given me a brochure on seaside resorts where I could escape for the week! I was becoming more bored by the minute! The leaflet narrated by Fr. Tomislav Vlasic, a Franciscan friar from Medjugorje explained briefly the background to Medjugorje which like every other parish in Western Herzegovina was mostly Catholic and with a strong traditional faith. According to Fr. Vlasic who ministers to the Catholic people, they were already on the road to a declining faith. Many young people did not go to the church to pray and fewer families were praying the Rosary at home.

According to this leaflet the parish had 2,500[11] inhabitants. He wrote about the phenomenon of Our Lady appearing on 24th June 1981 to six villagers and how one of the visionaries sprinkled holy water on Our Lady, saying: "I sprinkle you with holy water; if you are from Satan go away; if you are from God stay with us." Our Lady smiled and said: "I am the Virgin Mary." The rest of the leaflet contained messages on peace, prayer, penance, fasting, as well as information on extraordinary phenomenal happenings at Medjugorje. These included occurrences such as secret messages apparently given to the visionaries by the Virgin Mary; unusual writings and shapes observed in the sky and two visionaries' experiences of inner locution[12] received from Mary. It also described the conversion of the local parish in Medjugorje from apathy towards God to a deep commitment to their faith.

11 Now 5,000 inhabitants.

12 The best way I have heard an Inner Locution described: a phenomenon experience of hearing and seeing an interior vision, similar to viewing a film interiorly.

The fruits of the conversion of the village were the numerous prayer groups springing up all over the world which had found their roots in Medjugorje. The leaflet also gave instructions on how to pray and reminded the reader that all are equal in the eyes of God and that the life of the Medjugorje parish was an example for the whole world.

There were two groups sharing our house in Medjugorje, our group and one from Dundalk, Ireland. We had a quick tour of the village before going to bed. I slept very poorly, wondering how I could get out of the place. The town of Mostar was half an hour away. Maybe I could go there? I decided to rise early to see the village in daylight. Outside the house, Nicky, the other group leader, gave me directions. I browsed at shop windows before returning for breakfast.

After breakfast, the group leader led us to Apparition Hill[13] where Our Lady apparently first appeared. We set off and I carried a tripod on my shoulder for Father Tracey, our Spiritual Director from Ireland. He was carrying a huge camera and equipment on his back. In his role as a producer from Kairos, a production company that showed religious programmes on Irish television, he was undertaking some film work in Medjugorje at that time.

Our group leader pointed out a much bigger hill in the distance, called Cross-Mountain[14] and explained that the two hills, and the Church of St. James formed a triangle like the Trinity – Father (Church), Son (Cross-Mountain) and Our Lady, Spouse of the Holy Spirit (Apparition Hill). We arrived at the village at the foot of Apparition Hill and our group leader pointed to a house where Vicka, the visionary, lived. We walked up Apparition Hill via the blue cross which is situated near the bottom of the hill and close to the village. Ivan, a visionary, erected the blue cross at a place where he could receive the apparitions from Our Lady as the police with dogs tried to prevent him climbing the hill.

13 The local name is Podbrdo: approximately 60ft.

14 The local name is Mount Krizevac: approximately 1,500ft.

I separated from the group and climbed the rest of the hill to the place where Our Lady apparently first appeared to the six visionaries. A large crowd appeared to be in deep and sincere prayer around a cross placed at the spot where Our Lady first appeared. I felt no desire to join them. When the rest of the group caught up, we were invited to pray in silence on the hill. I sat on a rock without praying and as I was bored to death I bounded off the hill to a bar in the village.

Then I met Nicky.

NICKY

I was sitting at a table on the pavement outside the bar when I saw Nicky, the man from Dundalk limping along the street in my direction. As he came closer I looked up and smiled at him. He sat beside me and we shook hands. Nicky told me that this was his fourth time in Medjugorje. "Maybe you can tell me how the hell I can get out of this place," I heard myself say. "I will be surprised if you say that by the end of the week," he responded. "In any case you are here to meet a woman," Nicky declared as he slapped me on the shoulder. Thinking he was referring to my single state and women generally I rejected that idea out of hand. I now know my mind was on a different wavelength to his!

Over drinks and coffee, I was expounding on my reason for falling away from the Catholic Faith but no matter what I said to Nicky he had an answer. He told me several stories including how his mother had great faith and was always praying the Rosary in the hope that he and his brother would return to their original Catholic denomination, as they both had become "Born Again Christians".

Nicky was paralysed on his left side from an early age. His parents had taken him to Lourdes[15] in the hope of a cure. On Nicky's last visit to Medjugorje he experienced a supernatural healing which he said was a gift from Our Lady. On returning home, full of excitement and great happiness after spending time in Medjugorje someone commented to him, "All we hear from you is Medjugorje, Medjugorje, Medjugorje, but it hasn't cured you!" Nicky replied instantly "It has cured me, here," pointing to his heart. The moment Nicky put his hand to his heart, all idea of leaving Medjugorje left me.

15 Place of Pilgrimage in France. Our Lady appeared to a young girl called Bernadette from February 11th to July 16th, 1858.

Coming from a man who had been paralysed for some forty-one years, this statement had a profound effect on me. It really humbled me and I needed to hear more! Only 24 hours earlier as he limped around Dublin Airport, my thoughts about him were, "That poor fellow is off to Medjugorje hoping for a cure" and "I probably spend more on a bottle of champagne than he receives in social benefit in a week!" Now he was telling me of an "inner healing" I never knew existed! I had to talk more with this man. It was as if he was sent by God especially to deal with my specific problems. Conversation with him reminded me of the relief I would experience in my earlier life when I confessed my sins to a priest but now it felt as if Nicky was fulfilling that same need for me by listening to me, but without the completion of absolution from a priest.

DAY TWO

The following morning we met at the house where two of the visionaries, Mirjana and Jakov were scheduled to speak. I listened very carefully to them as they told us about heaven, purgatory[16] and hell. Our Lady had apparently shown the children visions of heaven, purgatory and hell and they explained these supernatural phenomena in their words to us all. Heaven was very peaceful, full of happiness, and everyone looked the same age. Purgatory was a desolate place, grey, gloomy and covered in mist and they could only hear souls weeping and moaning, as if in great pain, but could not see them. Some of the visionaries, including Jakov, were shown a vision of hell but they found it so horrendous that they did not wish to talk about it. Vicka has said she saw people entering hell and coming out looking like animals. Our Lady had told them that very few people go directly to heaven because those dying were not prepared for death.

I wondered if all my friends who had died suddenly were prepared? I thought of the futility of the falling out with my brother and how I could have been with him in his last hours. If only I had known how long the "Supreme Surgeon" had given him to live I would have done things differently. The well-worn phrase "you never know the day or the hour" was very relevant now. The visionaries were spelling out the importance of always being prepared to meet God and to be at peace with one another. Mirjana and Jakov also described certain things that were offensive to Our Lady; divorce and abortion being the main ones I remember. I was aware that this helped me to examine my conscience in preparation for confession. Over the years I had fooled myself that nothing was sinful!

16 The name given to the place where those who die in God's grace and friendship go for a final purification, if it is needed.

DAY THREE

I set out at 6 am on my own for Apparition Hill and was praying the Rosary with beads in my hand for the first time in nearly forty years. Very soon my tears were flowing. I remember looking up to heaven and saying "God, I am an ex footballer and rugby player, I am much more macho than this, and this is not what I want!" I continued walking and praying but the tears kept flowing and at this point some very strange and inexplicable things happened.

The first incident that seemed very strange was when I passed a small field and was aware of two children who seemed to be playing football. As I drew closer, their movements appeared to be frozen in time, but at the same time they were smiling at me. It was 6.15 am and in hindsight, I realise that this was a very early and unusual time in the morning for any child to be playing football. Although I have since visited that spot several times since that morning, I have never come across these children or any other children at that time in the morning[17].

As I looked towards Apparition Hill, I was surprised to see that it appeared to have completely disappeared but Cross-Mountain was still in sight. St. James's Church, which should have been seen as reasonably near, appeared to be miles away. Of the three points of the Trinity (St. James's Church, Cross-Mountain and Apparition Hill) I could see only two (Cross-Mountain and the Church) but the church appeared to be miles away. I could see the canopy at the end of the church, the large open space and the benches that are used for open-air services.

During my walk that morning towards Apparition Hill and before I reached Cross-Mountain, I saw the same view from various different vantage points. Three days later I realised that the views experienced were what I would have seen if I were standing on the base of the cross on Cross Mountain which is some two miles away and 1,500 feet high. God graced me with a wonderful understanding of the Trinity through this mysterious experience.

17 See under heading, "New Charity" for further explanation.

Although I didn't meet or see anyone apart from the children on my walk, I heard a male voice whispering in my ear telling me to go right down a particular pathway. It was now around 6.45 am. As I progressed on this pathway, an old Middle-Eastern looking man wearing a light tan Arabic style dress and fez hat passed me, riding a motor scooter at what seemed to be an impossibly slow speed! I stared in amazement and wondered how he could stay upright. As I looked further on, I noticed a dozen or so people in a field, bent down with their arms flaying. They appeared to be picking things off the ground, but I couldn't determine what these were. Not one of them rose from that position. It all appeared to be out of the ordinary.[18]

At the time I felt all these strange happenings should have a normal local explanation, nevertheless I was very baffled. I had been very alert and was reasoning things out as I went along but nothing seemed to make sense. However, the path did lead me to the base of Cross-Mountain and I started to climb. At this time I had no idea that Cross-Mountain was known as the "Way of the Cross"[19] or that the pathway up the hill was lined with the Stations of the Cross.[20] Each one of these stations illustrated on bronze plaques Jesus' last moments in the world on his journey to his crucifixion at Golgotha;[21]

(1) Jesus is unjustly condemned to death by Pilate to die on the Cross,
(2) Jesus receives the cross for His crucifixion and carries it on His shoulders,
(3) Jesus, weakened by the guards striking Him, falls under the weight of the cross, the first time,
(4) Jesus is met on this journey by His mother Mary,
(5) Simon of Cyrene is commissioned to help Jesus carry His cross,
(6) Veronica, a holy woman wipes the face of Jesus bathed in sweat and blood with a towel,
(7) Jesus, falls a second time under the weight of the cross,
(8) The women of Jerusalem weep for Jesus, as He comforts them with His words,

18 See under heading, "New Charity" for further explanation.

19 Fourteen meditations on the journey Jesus took on Good Friday as he walked to his death on the Cross.

20 Fourteen meditations on the journey Jesus took on Good Friday as he walked to his death on the Cross.

21 The place of Jesus' crucifixion. (Skull) The Latin name "Calvarius" (bad skull) has been retained in the form "Calvary" (Luke 23:33) Golgotha was also a place of execution for all common criminals.

(9) Jesus falls for the third time as his executioners try to hasten His steps when He could hardly move,
(10) Jesus is violently stripped of His garments by His executioners,
(11) Jesus is nailed to the cross, and offers His life to His father for our salvation,
(12) Jesus dies on the cross after three hours of agony,
(13) Jesus is taken down from the cross by two of His disciples, Joseph and Nicodemus and placed in the arms of His Mother,
(14) Jesus is placed in the Sepulchre for burial by His disciples and His Mother, and they close the tomb and walk away[22].

I was turning left at the third Station of the Cross, which portrays Jesus falling for the first time, when I heard a crackling noise (like a branch breaking) coming from the bushes behind the bronze plaque. I looked back and the centre leaves in the bushes behind the bronze plaque were shimmering. I thought I could see a human face in the shimmering leaves. I was about to walk on but I turned back again and in the opening to the left of the still shimmering bush an old lady with a very sad face was waving at me with her right hand. As I walked on I looked back again and she was still waving, smiling slightly. I nodded and continued my journey to the summit and the cross, which is an eight metre high stone structure[23].

A lot of people were in deep prayer at the cross. I stretched over some people and very lightly touched the back of the cross and I then found a quiet place to pray the Rosary behind the cross. The tears started to flow again and I simply could not stop crying. When I finished praying I left the summit to go down to the area where I had seen the old lady earlier. There was no sign of her. I was about to leave when I heard her voice from further down the rocky terrain. "Who are you?" I said, "Are you the Mother of God?"[24]

22 Akers, G. 1993. The Stations of the Cross by St. Alphonsus

23 Built in 1933 after a delegation from Medjugorje had sought permission to build it from Pope Pius X1. The pope gave the project his blessing and also gave them a piece of "the true Cross" (the Cross that Jesus was crucified on) and this piece of wood was built into the crossbeam of this cross.

24 "This title of Mary was applied to her at the Council of Ephesus in 431 and confirmed at the Council of Chalcedon in 451". This divine motherhood is the source of all Mary's privileges and graces. It is the source of all honour that is given to her. Through the centuries, the Church has constantly avowed, as at the third Council of Constantinople, that Jesus Christ was born "of the Holy Spirit and the Virgin Mary, rightly and truly the Mother of God according to His humanity". Though the "Mother of God" is not found directly stated in the New Testament, similar terms are used, as when Elizabeth calls Mary the "Mother of my Lord," and as in Luke 1:32 where Mary's future Son is called "Son of the most high." (Bauer, J. 1999, p. 224)

Church and surroundings as seen from vineyards on day three

Cross Mountain

The triangle like the Trinity - Father (Church), Son (Cross-Mountain) and Our Lady Spouse of the Holy Spirit (Apparition Hill).

Apparition Hill, which disappeared from view on day three

*Pathway where
I saw the mid-eastern
looking gentleman
on a motor scooter*

*Local old lady on
Cross-Mountain*

St. James's Church

Mirjana during an apparition on 2nd of June 2004

'Emo Forever' winning at Cheltenham with jockey Mark Dwyer

'Realt Na Nona' winning at Wetherby with jockey Jonjo O'Neill

Arthur and Nicky

Fr. Slavko's Memorial Stone at the spot where he died on Cross-Mountain

The Grandparents home at Vionica, with one of the residents Ilija Kordic.

New Orphanage under construction at Novi Travnik, due for completion in 2007.

President Ivo Miro Jovic, presenting a map of his country and a medal of honour which I accepted on behalf of all our donors.

The first of sixty children to attend the new school in Kiseljak, near Sarajevo which brought great joy to everyone.

Sr. Jelenka Puljic, Mother Provincial and Sr. Janja co-ordinators of this beautiful project.

Children receiving love and affection in the Kindergarten School from Sisters Catherine and Sr. Lidija at Kiseljak.

Ornella Vucic has spent the last eleven years in a coma and has never seen her twin boys. (pictured below with family friend) Your prayers are invited for her.

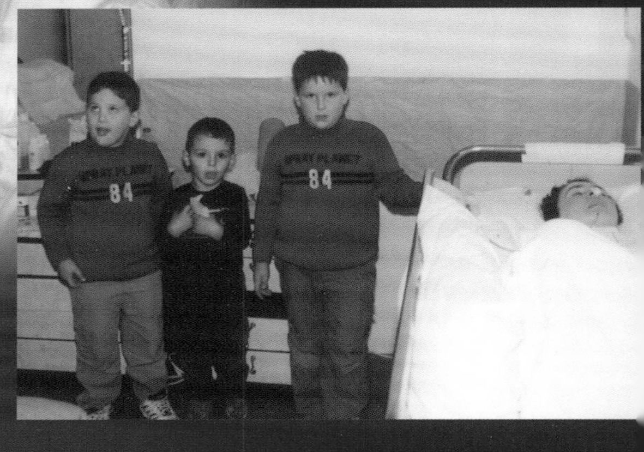

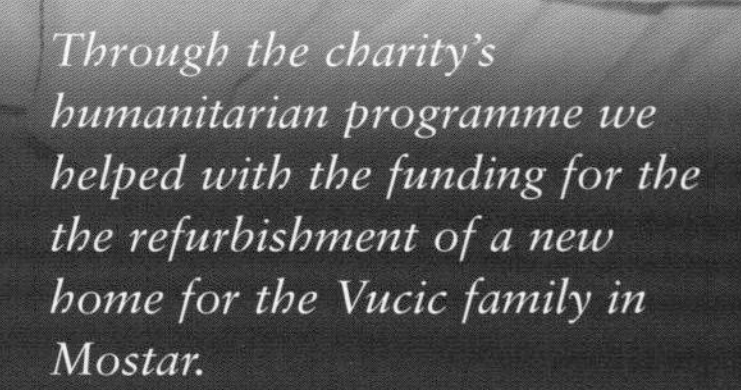

Through the charity's humanitarian programme we helped with the funding for the the refurbishment of a new home for the Vucic family in Mostar.

View of school at Kileljak from the playground with children at play time.

Kevin Leacy and friends from Gorey, Co. Wexford raised €20,000 at the Dublin City Marathon in aid of the Kindergarten School.

With arms outstretched she appeared to glide over the boulders and was in my arms in an instant. We were both crying and she invited me to sit down beside her. With both hands cupped she then made a beautiful presentation of several strings of Rosary Beads to me. These were replicas of the one I had received ten years earlier from Eleanor. They were all radiantly white except for one blue string of beads in the middle. I felt compelled to take the blue string of beads as I felt that these were a special gift to me from Our Lady. The old lady touched me on the shoulder and indicated in her language that we should pray for one another, me for her, she for me. The tears were flowing and I was crying loudly like a child.

I was staring at my feet trying to concentrate and I could see the numbers 666[25] on the lapels of my shoes. Instantly I experienced a feeling of dread and an awareness of a connection with Satan; a feeling exactly opposite to the love and goodness emanating out of the old woman. Had I been walking in Satan's shoes all my adult life? Only later on in Ireland after reading the Bible,[26] did I realise the significance of these numbers. During our prayers the old lady hung a knitted set of Rosary Beads around my neck on the outside of my shirt. After praying, she spoke in her own language and holding her sore leg, indicated that she had many problems. I had my arm around her shoulder to console her and kissed her on the cheek. I said I had many problems also but mine were spiritual. She probably did not understand me, but we hugged one another and with my parting words "be happy" I left with only one thing on my mind, to find a priest as quickly as possible in order to confess my sins and seek absolution. I felt deep down something absolutely wonderful had happened to me.

Afterwards I discovered that the old lady was a local woman but through whom I felt I had received many of God's graces[27]. The priests were not hearing confessions until evening. I had to wait all day and I felt my resolve weaken. I confided this to Nicky and he became a tower of strength, supporting me until I reached the safety of the priest.

25 The mark of the Beast (thought to be Satan) as found in Scripture (Revelations 13:18).

26 Revelations 13:18.

27 Any undeserved gift or help freely and lovingly provided by God, but above all the utterly basic gift of being saved in Christ through faith, a grace that God wishes to give to all human beings (O'Collins and Farrugia, 2000, p. 98)

That evening, having made a list of my sins on a piece of paper during the day, I went straight to confession. On the way I quietly prayed, asking Mary, our Mother in Heaven, to help me. There was a long queue outside the confessional box and I seemed to be waiting for a long time. Everyone appeared to take ages to confess his or her sins. I felt a strong urge to leave. I reasoned with myself that there was plenty of time to go to confession the next day. I very nearly did a bunk! It felt as if Satan was perhaps quietly prompting me, telling me to leave, trying to keep me in my state of sin. It was almost as if he was not going to give up on me too easily. After all I had been a model pupil of sin for years. Somehow, I found the strength to stay and enter the confessional box[28].

Once inside the confessional box, face to face with the Priest who was going to hear my confessions, I took off my dark glasses and said, "Father[29], it is over twenty years since I last went to confession". He simply said, "Welcome, how are you, what line of business are you in?" All the apprehension I had felt beforehand left me and I immediately relaxed in the presence of this lovely man. We had a great chat. I told him about my experience of meeting the old lady on Cross-Mountain and how this led me to realising my need for repentance". His warm handshake and kindly smile at the end were such a tonic that I left the confessional on cloud nine to do the penance[30] for the sins I had confessed to him, in atonement to God.

My spiritual life had been changed, transformed dramatically only three days after my arrival in Medjugorje. As far as I was concerned I was in heaven on earth and I was not looking forward to leaving! I told Nicky about my conversion experience and we embraced with joy. He said, he would climb Cross-Mountain as a special thanks to Jesus for my conversion.

28 A cubicle or a room where the penitent goes to the priest to confess.

29 Title Catholics give to their priests.

30 In order to facilitate the conversion from sin to God, the sinner must have a deep need to confess sin, receive pardon from God and be reconciled with the community harmed by our sins. This can be facilitated through prayer, fasting, giving alms to the poor or doing some good work. (O'Collins and Farrugia, 2000, p. 196).

DAY FOUR

We heard more talks from the visionary Ivan and he says that Our Lady's messages to the world are simple. She asks us to get closer to God and to convert through prayer, peace, fasting and penance. She starts each message, "Dear Children" and in doing so she is addressing each one of us regardless of colour or religion. All are equal in God's eyes and it is His responsibility, not ours, to judge others.

I climbed the Cross-Mountain for the second time with Nicky and the group. A priest said afterwards that half his group had felt they could not make it to the top but Nicky had pulled them all the way up with his example. It was very humbling knowing that the super human effort he was making was on my behalf. It was a reminder of the monumental effort Jesus made for all of us by dying on the cross so that our sins would be forgiven. I was re-living every step that Jesus took on his final journey and my heart went out to His Mother for the pain she must have endured in witnessing those painful and cruel scenes of Jesus carrying His cross to Golgotha and then being crucified. I was looking after Nicky's needs with water and towel, reminding me a little of Simon and Veronica; Simon had helped Jesus carry His cross and Veronica offered Jesus a towel to wipe his face.

I admired the priests on our pilgrimage and the way their prayers made the "Way of the Cross" so real as we traversed our way up the hill to the top from one station to the next. It was explained to us that in 1933 a delegation from Medjugorje had gone to Rome to seek permission from Pope Pius XI to build the cross on Cross-Mountain. Not only did the Pope give them permission to do so, he also gave them a piece of "the true cross" (from the cross that Jesus was crucified on) and this was built into the crossbeam of the cross on Cross-Mountain. I never felt so close or so in love with Jesus as I did then. On the way down I stopped to pray the Rosary in the area behind the third Station of the Cross and enjoyed the peaceful tranquillity of the spot where my conversion started twenty-four hours earlier.

DAY FIVE

We had a wonderful experience the following day with a visit to the visionary Vicka's home to hear more of Our Lady's messages. Vicka was the one who threw the holy water at Our Lady and invited her to leave if she was from Satan. Later we visited Father Jozo Zovko at his parish church some forty-five minutes away in Siroki Brijeg for his afternoon of prayer. He was the parish priest in Medjugorje when the apparitions first started. Father Jozo did not believe in the apparitions to begin with and this suited the Communist regime. However, he later saw Our Lady in an apparition who assured him that the children were telling the truth. This changed his heart and because of this change, the communists jailed him on account of his belief in the children and in the apparitions. Prior to being jailed, it was under his spiritual direction that the parish of Medjugorje was brought to the point of reconciliation through prayer and fasting. That evening in Medjugorje the Croatian Army paraded to the church for a dedication ceremony to Our Lady. Each soldier carried a red or blue candle and wore blue sashes. These colours represent the Croatian National Flag. It was a wonderful spectacle led by Father Slavko Barbaric[31].

31 A parish priest in Medjugorje who died suddenly in 2000.

DAY SIX

The following morning, three of us set out at 5 am for Apparition Hill. Again I was very humbled at the supreme effort made by Nicky in climbing this smaller hill. The way down is much more difficult for him to negotiate with loose stones proving a major problem. Nicky related that Our Lady had touched him the year before at a particular spot on the hill. He demonstrated how he had fallen on his right side and looked over at Cross-Mountain and said, "Jesus there is no way I will be seeing you tomorrow." With that, he felt as if an invisible hand was gently grabbing him by his paralysed left arm and leading him to the base of the hill. He did climb Cross-Mountain the next day.

I went off on my own to climb Cross-Mountain for the third time, along the same route as I had taken three days earlier. From the same vantage points as before, Apparition Hill was visible again (out of vision three days earlier). St. James's Church and surrounding details (also very clear three days earlier) had now practically disappeared, with only the tips of the twin spires visible over the trees and the view from the top of the mountain had returned to normal. On Cross-Mountain near the fourteenth station an inner voice told me, "you will be on the cross on your own," which seemed impossible as the place was so crowded. Soon I found myself at the summit and at the foot of the stone cross on my own. Everyone seemed to have melted away. I bent forward and placed both hands on the top of the altar (incorporated into the base of the cross) and heard myself say, *"Jesus I am yours forever."* The altar appeared to come alive in my hands and it was as if I was feeling flesh. I was aware of hearing what appeared to be a very deep male voice coming from the cross praying an act of contrition over me. A sensation came right up through my body starting down at my feet and coming up to my chest.

I stood up, perfectly calm, with a great sensation of peace in my heart. I looked down from the summit of Cross-Mountain to St. James's Church, and in terms of vista and distance the picture was exactly as I had seen it three days earlier when I was standing in the vineyards in close proximity to the church. I felt that Our Lady on Apparition Hill had led me to her Son on Cross-Mountain and in turn He had pointed me to His Father in the church. I prayed the Rosary at the cross, peacefully enjoying the fantastic beauty of the valley.

I returned once again to where I had my conversion experience at the Third Station. I lingered prayerfully for an hour not wishing to leave as I felt I was in heaven on earth. My reluctance at going to Medjugorje to begin with had now turned full circle in that I did not wish to leave. On our return journey to Dublin I invited Nicky to return with me to Medjugorje in September, as our group leader. I was determined to return as soon as possible with family and friends.

WITNESSING

A FURTHER TRIP

WITNESSING

On my return to Glasgow I told all my close friends about Medjugorje and how it was a place of spiritual uplift for all religions. Apart from the spiritual aspect there is also a lovely, relaxed atmosphere, which lends itself to plenty of social interaction. I told them about my strong feelings about returning to live in Ireland. I explained about promises I had made to my mother and that my heart was telling me the time had come to fulfil these promises. I also felt strongly inspired to play a role through young people in promoting Medjugorje. As yet I do not know how this will be manifested but I have every confidence that it will happen. I wrote to various people including members of my own family expressing regret for earlier confrontations asking for forgiveness.

My parish priest in Glasgow could not believe his eyes when I started attending daily mass! I told him I had a story to tell him sometime and two days later he arrived at my home. He said his curiosity had got the better of him! He was fascinated to hear my story but quickly found out that he was losing a changed parishioner! In any case he nearly knew my mother better than myself because the only time he would see me at church was when she came over from Ireland to Scotland on holiday! I eventually returned to live with my mother in Portarlington to fulfil promises I had made to her in earlier life. I am semi-retired with some business interests in Scotland and this takes me back there a couple of times per month. When I finally left Scotland, in October 1999, after thirty-five years living there, I found it very hard to say goodbye to my friends in Glasgow.

A FURTHER TRIP

I could not wait to get back to Medjugorje and twelve weeks later I returned with seven people, four of my family, including my mother and three friends of long standing. My niece, who married in February 1999, came all the way from Houston in Texas. Prior to going she asked, "Arthur can you guarantee me there is an after life?" I replied that before my visit to Medjugorje in June 1999 I did not believe in God or eternal life but now I could guarantee one hundred percent that He does exist and that there is an afterlife. Her conversion in September 1999 bears witness to her new found beliefs.

Later in the week my mother and I went to confessions to Father Svet. At the end of her confession Father Svet aided her out of the confessional box on his arm in true gentlemanly fashion. He was singing her praises to me when I entered the confessional box. "What faith that woman has", he proclaimed. I told him she was my mother and I was so proud that she could come with me to Medjugorje. I told him that he had been my confessor when I converted three months previously. He asked if I was attending mass regularly and smiled when I told him that I tried to attend daily. He then heard my confession and after absolution he shook my hand. Clutching on to his hand I told him about my profound spiritual experience at the foot of the cross on Cross-Mountain. With eyes closed, this conduit of the Holy Spirit told me that it was my mother's faith which was coming through the cross for me, my family and friends and I was to leave it at that.

Other highlights of the week included a meeting with the visionary Mirjana. We had a talk from Father Slavko Barbaric on Our Lady's messages[32] and their meaning through prayer, peace, penance and fasting. This time I visited the Cenacolo Community[33] for recovering addicts (one opened in Knock[34], Ireland in 1999) and we heard from two of the addicts about their lives and hopes for the future. Sr. Elvira, the foundress of the community believes that Jesus is the only one who can heal us totally. There is no medication, so work and prayer are the foundations of community life. Each addict is assigned a "Guardian Angel" on his or her arrival into the community, someone who is also an addict, who has walked the path of recovery previously and who understands the complex difficulties and trials of the recovering addict. For those who stay, there is a high success rate, but the time spent in community can be from three to five years whilst the young men and women learn how to live a new way of life, free from drugs, alcohol and other toxic substances and addictions.

32 Given on the 25th of each month to one of the visionaries, generally calling on us to pray and fast more for her intercessions.

33 Cenacalo Community – http://www.campo-della-vita.org/inglesa/index(ing).htm

34 Marian Shrine in Ireland where Our Lady appeared to 15 people on the 21st August 1879. (http://www.knock-shrine.ie/).

GAMBLING
ALCOHOL ADDICTION

GAMBLING

I mentioned earlier of my gambling addiction and that during my first week in Medjugorje I prayed for a cure from this dreadful illness. I had tried for many years to give it up. In sheer desperation and on many occasions, I telephoned the "gamblers anonymous"[35] charity number seeking help. The response was always a recorded message inviting me to leave my particulars stating that someone would get back to me. I never did, always putting the phone down convincing myself that I could defeat the illness myself. My best effort not to gamble lasted nine weeks but generally when I did gamble, it was only a matter of days before the addiction kicked in. Concerned friends never heard the truth from me. Addiction makes the addict a dreadful liar. I could never tell the truth about how much I was winning or losing. To do so would have revealed the level of my betting. The truth was never an option, as I felt ashamed of my lack of control and destructive way of life.

I did not become a gambling addict when I was wealthy and owned horses. In hindsight it happened before I was twelve years of age when I had my first ever bet on the 1956 English Grand National. I backed my hero, a jockey named Pat Taffee to win the race on a prized horse, Quare Times. With eyes closed I put a pin in the rest of the field and picked out a horse named Tudor Line. Quare Times won and Tudor Line finished second! Backing the first and second in the greatest race in the world was surely an easy way to make money! Alas, this was not to be the case.

Some months later I stole £40 (a very considerable sum of money at the time) from the home of my family's best friends, which I had every intention of replacing, but the scheme to make my fortune went badly wrong.

35 A fellowship of men and women who have joined together to do something about their gambling problem and to help other compulsive gamblers to do the same.
Telephone numbers: Ireland: 01 8721133; 091 565207; UK National 08700 50 88 80; London: 020 7384 3040; Sheffield: 0114 262 0026; Manchester; 0161 976 5000; Birmingham: 0121 233 1335; Glasgow; 0141 630 1033; Belfast: 028 7135 1329 or http://www.gamblersanonymous.org.uk/. Links: Australia – www.gamblersanonymous.org.au: Canada (Edmonton area) www.edmontonga.com; USA – www.gamblersanonymous.org

The horses I backed all lost. The money was missed and as a regular visitor to our friend's home I expressed great concern that anyone should do such a thing. I denied any possibility that I was the guilty one and even suggested someone else as the probable culprit. However, when the Garda (Police) were called I admitted my guilt. I will never forget the shame I brought on my parents and the worry of it all nearly killed my father. When I went up to his bedroom to apologise he was lying in bed exhausted and hyperventilating from the worry of it all. Since the family I stole the money from would not press charges the case against me was dropped.

I was too young at the time to fully appreciate the charity that family showed in instantly forgiving me for my foolishness. They are a beautiful family with great Christian values and thank God they are my best friends to this day. After this incident I never stole again, but instead, as a youth, worked hard for local farmers to earn money which invariably ended up with the bookmakers!

Over the years there were some good days when I won large amounts of money and had a "ball" enjoying these occasions. However, when a person is a compulsive gambler it is impossible to win long term. Regardless of how wealthy the person is, once he or she backs a loser, a little man in the head is pushing for those losses to be recovered and in many cases I was telephoning bets until the last race of the day was over. At the end of the day I felt shattered with a huge sense of guilt for being so stupid and of course swearing never to do the same again. I was a good businessman, but I became a complete fool with money when the compulsive streak kicked in. I was a single person doing considerable damage financially to myself, but many a happy family with a gambling addict in their midst, is completely destroyed. For approximately three years after my conversion in Medjugorje there were occasions when I was tempted to gamble. I somehow always managed to resist these temptations and I can now say that the days of trying to beat the bookmakers are over for me. I thank God for listening to my prayers.

ALCOHOL ADDICTION

I never thought of myself as an "alcoholic." I certainly loved to drink and perhaps I could describe myself as a "social alcoholic." I lost my driving licence twice for drinking and driving (one year and three years off the road) but it could have happened a thousand times. Most of us were drinking and driving in those days but thank God no one was hurt during some of my mad escapades behind the wheel. However, since my experience of the cross on Cross-Mountain coming alive in my hands I have never had a desire or taste for alcohol since. I asked God for a healing from my gambling addiction and in His goodness, He not only did so, but healed me from alcohol as well. The healing that took place cannot effectively be explained in words; it needs to be fully experienced to be understood. Praise and glory to God for these wonderful miracles in my life.

I start every day with a prayer to the Holy Spirit for His guidance. Every day I pray to the Immaculate Heart[36] of Our Blessed Mother to thank her for pointing me in the direction of her son Jesus. I also pray daily to the Sacred Heart[37] of Jesus to thank him for pointing me in the direction of his Father in the Church, for the peace, contentment and happiness He has brought to my life and for the courage to be a witness in His name. I also pray in a special way for others and if you desire prayers for any reason, please do not hesitate to write or e-mail me with details and I will include your intentions in my daily prayers. I also need and ask you to remember me in your prayers.

36 "A devotion fostered by John Eudes in seventeenth-century France through his book " The Admirable Heart of Mary" and re-popularised on account of the apparitions of Mary at Fatima, Portugal in 1917. On the 25th anniversary of Fatima, Pius XII consecrated the whole human race to the Immaculate Heart of Mary and he extended the feast of the Immaculate Heart of Mary to the whole Church. This devotion recognises the Heart as the symbol of her maternal love, which assented wholeheartedly to Jesus Christ, His coming and His Redemption. Such love from Mary draws us closer to Christ". (Bauer, J. 1999, p. 214).

37 Jesus has always loved us through His entire life even when our sins pierced His heart. He willingly became the sacrificial lamb and suffered the agony of knowing that He was going to be crucified, in order that He could pay for our sins and so that we would find salvation and eternal life. For this reason, His heart, which has shown to us a divine love and a human love, is known as the Sacred Heart. The "Sacred Heart of Jesus" has therefore become the sign and symbol of that wonderful love.

MY MOTHER'S DEATH

MY MOTHER'S DEATH

One of the greatest gifts God granted me was to be with my mother during the last two years of her life. She was eighty-seven years old when I returned home to live with her and by then she was dependent on others to chauffeur her to Sunday Mass and to undertake her daily shopping. She was a wonderful mother and a very gifted cook. We had many a laugh together about her acceptance of the falling standards in that department, as she now had to contend with my limited cooking ability! However, she never once complained and ate every meal!

Taking her on a pilgrimage to Medjugorje was very special but to be with her at Mass[38] on Sundays was a real joy. She knew the Mass inside out and since I was still very much on a learning curve, I learned all the prayers from listening to her. It was also a special joy to kneel down in our home at night to pray the Rosary together. Many times I arrived home late after giving a testimony[39] of my conversion to some prayer group but she was always waiting for me to pray the Rosary before going to bed. I treasure these wonderful times together and also her sharing of many personal and private matters with me.

In August 2001 she became unwell. At that time Radio Telefis Eireann (RTE; Irish Television) wished to do a programme on my conversion experience and also the work I was involved with, for the Charity Rebuild for Bosnia,[40] for their "Would You Believe" series. It was to be filmed in Medjugorje during September or October 2001 but because of my mother's illness I could not go. The family expected her to pass away during this time but Mama's health picked up and she was well enough to participate in her ninetieth birthday party on November 9th, which the family lovingly organised. We celebrated Mass in the house and it was an occasion that will never be forgotten.

38 A Catholic prescribed form of public worship in celebration of the "Eucharist". The "Eucharist" was instituted by Christ at the Last Supper (bread and wine; body and blood) and represents the new covenant. This begins with the gathering of the Christians and always includes: the proclamation of the Word of God; thanksgiving to God the Father for all his benefits, above all the gift of his son; the consecration of bread and wine; participation in the liturgical banquet by receiving the Lord's body and blood. These elements constitute one single act of worship CCC 1408).

39 A true account of a happening.

40 Charity set up in Ireland to build homes for families who lost their home due to ethnic cleansing.

RTE then telephoned to say that if the filming could not be done early January 2002 it would be cancelled. Mama had weakened considerably by that time but was being lovingly cared for by three of my sisters. I made the decision to go. It was a wrench for me to leave Ireland for Medjugorje but I felt it would benefit the Charity to carry on with the filming. It was heart breaking saying goodbye to Mama as I felt sure that she would not survive the next eight days. She asked where I was going? When I said Medjugorje her whole face lit up with a most beautiful smile and then there was complete silence. We both knew it was our final parting and I told her I would pray for her to Our Blessed Mother in Medjugorje. I then left with a very heavy heart.

During the stay in Medjugorje every time my mobile telephone rang I was expecting bad news and each time I telephoned home I was expecting the worst. I was on tenter hooks all the time. The night before the final shoot, Patricia Keane (Chairperson of the Charity) and I were invited to witness the visionary, Marija, apparently receiving an apparition. The Rosary was being said beforehand but I could not put two words of the prayer together. All I could think of was "What in the name of God am I doing here, I should be at home with my dying mother?" Then the moment Marija went into ecstasy[41] I found myself offering my mother up to Our Blessed Mother for the wonderful mother she was and I asked Our Lady to look after her for me in Heaven. My heart was full of love for Mama.

The final filming was completed on Apparition Hill under the statue of Our Lady at the exact spot where she apparently first appeared in June 1981. After the interview the producer announced "We have a programme" and standing up I noticed our Croatian Director, Ante Muzic walking towards us. Thinking he was coming for the filming, I said, "Ante, you are too late. The filming is over." He told me that my sister had telephoned him and I was to telephone home. I did so and at the exact spot where Our Blessed Mother first appeared to the six Visionaries I learned of my mother's death.

41 A trance-like state.

I felt as if Our Blessed Mother had put her mantle over my shoulder in preparation for the news I most dreaded hearing. The three Directors of Rebuild for Bosnia and the four-crew members from RTE said the Glorious Mysteries[42] of the Rosary at the statue and it was a very moving experience.

Some twenty minutes later we delivered a wedding gift to Vicka, the visionary. Vicka ran out of the house and threw her arms around me smiling broadly and told me that my mother was in Heaven. I was overcome with delight and thanked God that she had received her just rewards for many years of loyalty to prayer. After that I never grieved her passing away but I miss her dearly. She was ninety years old, the branch was withering, she was ready to go having lived a very good life. I thank God for her life and for leaving me with such beautiful memories of a wonderful mother.

42 A mystery is a sacred thing, which is difficult to understand. The works of Our Lord and His Blessed Mother can be rightly called mysteries because they are so full of wonders and deep and sublime truths which the Holy Spirit reveals to each one of us who pray. The third part of the Rosary contains five mysteries, which are called the "Glorious Mysteries" because when we say them we meditate on Jesus and Mary in their triumph and glory. The first is the Resurrection of Jesus Christ; the second, His Ascension into heaven; the third, the Descent of the Holy Spirit upon the Apostles; the fourth, Our Lady's Assumption into heaven; the fifth, Our lady's crowing in heaven (De Montfort, L, 1954, p. 55).

FRUITS

NEW CHARITY

RECONCILIATION

TESTIMONY

FRUITS

When I returned to live with my mother in Ireland in October 1999, I made the journey by boat from Troon to Belfast. During that journey, I felt as if I was being prompted through my heart to set up a charity. The prompting was so real that I instantly started to form the charity in my mind. However, after thirty-five years away from Ireland I could not even come up with the name of one person I could ask to be a Director in such a venture. Where was God leading me?

In November 1999 I started to write about my conversion experience in Medjugorje. Early in January 2000 a friend introduced me to a Spiritual Director for guidance and spiritual advice on what I had written. He was most helpful. Through prayer and guidance over the following weeks it was decided that I should now share my testimony with others. I was invited to do so by several prayers groups.

Sometime later, my Spiritual Director telephoned me to say he had recommended my testimony to Patricia Keane from a charity, Rebuild for Bosnia. Patricia and her fellow Directors in the charity had invited Wayne Weible[43] to Ireland to speak at several venues. This was to enable them to help raise funds to build houses for the victims of war in Bosnia & Herzegovina. Patricia was looking for someone locally with a conversion story. I had read some of Wayne's books telling of his own conversion story at Medjugorje and I was most impressed by his experiences. I was terrified at the idea of speaking alongside Wayne. That first night in Ballina, Co. Mayo, when we were both due to speak to a group, I felt extremely anxious. However, Wayne could not have been nicer and was most helpful in supporting me with his kind advice.

43 American speaker on Our Lady of Medjugorje.

At the end of a two-week tour of engagements with Patricia Keane and her fellow Directors, Patricia invited me to become a Director of Rebuild for Bosnia. The idea of giving a homeless family a new home was for me the ultimate in charity and I was delighted to accept. I felt that this must be what God had in mind for me and from the beginning of working with the charity, I felt very happy and totally committed to the work. I worked for the charity for four years and spent most of my time raising funds to re-house the ethnically cleansed families of the war in Bosnia-Herzegovina. By 2004, the Charity had built some seventy homes and had helped over six hundred people in the process. I resigned my Directorship at the end of March 2004 to establish another charity, "St. Joseph & The Helpers Charity Ltd."

NEW CHARITY

When I was aged fifteen or sixteen years, my mother and I won a prize playing bridge at the local golf club. It was a framed print of the head and shoulders of an old bearded unnamed man in a tan outfit. I hung it in my bedroom in Emo[44] and then later in Portarlington[45] and it remained there for all the years I was living in Scotland. I had no idea who the old gentleman was but he did have a saintly looking face. Over the years, on visits home in Ireland, I occasionally took notice of the picture. The only thoughts that ever came to mind about the picture, were "how lucky we were that night to win a prize!" My bridge game can be more than erratic at the best of times and my mother must have played brilliantly!

On returning home to live permanently in Ireland my first thought when seeing the picture again was that the old gentleman looked very like the person I saw riding the motor scooter on day three of my first pilgrimage to Medjugorje. Afterwards it crossed my mind that the old man might be St. Joseph. The slow speed he was travelling at that morning was similar to the speed of a donkey at walking pace. Was my imagination working overtime? However, some months later I had a meeting with my Spiritual Director in Dublin and whilst browsing at the back of the Church I noticed the original painting of my print and the name St. Joseph was written on it in the artist's writing! I did feel a great sense of excitement that my initial instincts were correct but I had no indication whatsoever that I was to act on them.

44 In County Laois, Ireland.
45 In Co. Laois/Offaly, Ireland.

However, some three years later I began to have continual flash backs of the man on the motor scooter, the workers in the field and the boys playing football. I felt a strong need for spiritual guidance on the matter and arranged a meeting with my Spiritual Director. On the morning of the meeting I was trying to put an agenda together in my mind as to why I had asked for the meeting in the first place

My mind was a total blank and I could not think of one reason for calling the meeting. Praying to the Holy Spirit for guidance it then came through my heart to talk to him about forming another charity. After the meeting, my Spiritual Director said that he also felt that I was being guided down another path and advised constant prayer to the Holy Spirit before our next meeting. Since then, I have always prayed to the Holy Spirit. After another meeting with my Spiritual Director, I felt compelled to start a new charity. The Charity, "St. Joseph & The Helpers Charity Ltd." has been established since 19th May 2004. Slowly the Charity has grown and it is now registered in Ireland, the United Kingdom and United States of America.[46]

46 (Website: www.helperscharity.com).

RECONCILIATION

My own life and attitudes have changed considerably since Medjugorje. I have a spiritual strength, which has given me a contentment that my friends recognise visually. I try to practise the messages of Our Lady through prayer, peace, penance and fasting. Reading the Bible has become a daily routine and I am also catching up on other interesting books, especially about Medjugorje, other Marian Shrines and conversion stories! In conclusion I would like to share a little story about confession from Sister Briege McKenna's book, "Miracles Do Happen".[47]

It relates to her vision of the beautiful garden with many flowers and among these flowers were little weeds. The Lord said to her, "Briege, this is your soul." The flowers represented the virtues she was trying to cultivate in her efforts to become holy. However, at the same time, as she walked around the garden admiring the flowers, she was looking at the weeds and saying, "Oh, they're just small and they won't do a bit of harm." She saw herself giving the weeds a little pat saying, "I'll not bother with you. You're just little weeds." Then the Lord said to her, "Those weeds represent sin. You are comparing yourself with the world, with all the evil in the world. You must never accept sin."

The gardener then comes in and said, "If you let me, I'll eradicate those weeds for you. Then the flowers will have a brighter colour and there will be greater growth in your garden."

47 McKenna Sr. B. (1987) page 26

God's forgiveness in confession, graced through Father Svet and the authority of the Church has done wonders for me. Our faulty attitudes to life can inadvertently create sinful situations. Regular confession helps to remove the roots of our sin and is a sacrament[48] I will not neglect in future. Yes, I can now believe that Medjugorje is indeed about conversion and confession.

I have many people to thank for my conversion and for helping me on the way. I am especially grateful to Our Lady and for her use of Nicky Hughes and the local "old lady" the powerful instrument of my conversion on Cross-Mountain.

48 (Lat. "public pledge of fidelity") A visible sign, instituted by Christ, which reveals and communicates grace. The Catholic Church and the Orthodox accept seven such sacraments: baptism, confirmation, Eucharist, marriage, holy orders, anointing of the sick, and penance (O'Collins and Farrugia, p. 231).

TESTIMONY

Since my conversion I have been invited to give my testimony on many occasions at conferences, to prayers groups, in schools and churches and I will continue to witness in this way. So far, at the time of writing in May 2007, I have been to Medjugorje over forty times. For many years I took groups three or four times a year and on other occasions I visit Medjugorje and work all week for the new charity. I have witnessed many new conversions through spiritual and physical healings that have made profound changes to people's lives. When Nicky pointed to his heart and told me he was cured there, he was talking about an inner healing that I never knew existed. This comment kept me in Medjugorje and when the healing of my own heart came, I fully understood the importance of that simple statement. Nicky said it in such a way that it seemed to diminish the importance of being partially crippled for forty years. Like Nicky, I am also convinced that healing of the heart is everything and that it leaves the person well prepared to carry out God's Will on Earth.

A visit to Medjugorje is something I cannot recommend too highly. Go with an open heart and let Our Blessed Mother take care of your needs.

A PRODIGAL SPEAKS

I sought the pleasures
That man seeks,
Ignored the urge
That cautioned care.

Unleashed the demons
Of my mind,
Dismissed the signs
That said beware.

I shared a carousel
With wings
With friends-who played
When stakes were high.
My world was vast
Immeasurable
Enclosed by contrails
In the sky.

Until I walked
"Between the Hills,"
Discovered Peace
This world can't give,
Discovered Love of One
Who died for me,
Upon a cross
That we might live.

Raymond McGreevy
Monaghan, Ireland

ST. JOSEPH & THE HELPERS CHARITY LTD

The main objective of the charity is to raise funds for the people of Bosnia & Herzegovina:

- To sponsor the support of children currently living in orphanages
- To provide poverty relief and humanitarian aid for education, healthcare and housing.
- To provide educational support and facilities for children and young adults.
- To support institutions which house broken families including orphaned children, young, middle-aged and the elderly.
- To support the mentally ill, disabled and elderly who have been abandoned in institutions.
- To support those who suffer from drug abuse and human rights abuses.

The charity views education as one of the most effective ways of helping to create a future for the youth of Bosnia & Herzegovina. The first project we were asked to support was the building of a Kindergarten School for 150 children in Kiseljak, near Sarajevo. I wrote earlier (page 36) about having strong feelings that I might help young people; perhaps they are coming to fruition some seven years later through my involvement with the Kindergarten project! Work started on site in May 2005 and everyone involved in the project was overjoyed when the first 60 children commenced their education in the school in January 2006. At the time of writing the charity has raised in excess of €500,000 for this project and all six classrooms are now completed, allowing the remaining 90 children to start their school lives in the near future.

The school building provides a meeting place for social activity for parents in an area where some 90% are unemployed and where no other social amenities exist. Through this project, it is expected that 16 people will eventually be employed and this will be a great boost for the local economy. The charity will continue to raise funds for the school, to provide staff salaries and to cover all the running costs.

Two other major building projects are underway. In Vionica, Medjugorje, a fifty-bed nursing home is now operational although not fully completed. This has been built for the grandparents of children living in a nearby orphanage who lost both parents during the war. There are currently 19 elderly people in the home, receiving loving and caring attention from Sr. Kornelija and her staff. We hope to complete this project before the end of 2007 together with the completion of the orphanage in Novi Travnik for 20 children and 5 staff.

The charity has been asked to become involved with the refurbishment of an existing Home for the mentally ill/physically handicapped people in Pazaric, near Sarajevo. There are some 300 residents, including many children and the condition of the building is extremely poor. Toilet conditions are completely unsanitary, with only one toilet available for every 70 patients. The Visionary, Jakov, has asked the charity for help and we are currently establishing the costs involved through local builders. Jakov and one of the other five Visionaries visit the Home on a regular basis to help with normal daily chores. Intentionally, they have not disclosed their identity to the staff or residents of the home.

Our humanitarian work involves us in beautiful and rewarding work. The provision of a new buggy to Lucija from Mostar, who suffered brain damage at birth, was a great joy for her family and has greatly enhanced all their lives.

Vjekoslav & Ornella Vucic married in Mostar some twelve years ago. A year later Ornella gave birth to twin boys, Kresimir and Domogoj. One was born at 5 minutes to midnight and the other 10 minutes later. Sadly, Ornella has never seen her children. She went into a coma during childbirth and 11 years later is still in the same condition and is being cared for by the Franciscan Nuns in a hospital in Mostar. God willing she will recover soon and be re-united with her loving family in the comfort of the new home, which the Municipality of Mostar provided and the charity refurbished at a cost in excess of €8,000.

In the summers of 2005 & 2006 we joined forces with Miracles Charity and paid for 60 orphaned children to have a week's holiday at the seaside. None of the children had ever seen the sea before and it was a wonderful holiday for all of them.

Our footwear programme, described by Fr. Svetozar as "one of the most basic requirement that children are desperately in need of" is receiving great support. We need the funds to purchase the shoes locally, which will also help the local economy.

Our programme to sponsor a child in an orphanage is gaining momentum and please God our appeal will continue to touch people's hearts. We have around seven hundred children, young people and staff to support in orphanages throughout Bosnia & Herzegovina. There is no state aid available in these areas; work is extremely hard to find and these proud people are in desperate need of your help.

In the Holy Bible, (Matthew 6: 1-4), Jesus gives the following teaching on alms giving:

"Take care not to perform righteous deeds in order that people may see them; otherwise, you will have no recompense from your heavenly Father. When you give alms, do not blow a trumpet before you, as the hypocrites do in the streets to win praise of others. Amen, I say to you, they have received their reward. But when you give alms, do not let your left hand know what your right hand is doing, so that alms giving may be secret. And your Father who sees in secret will repay you".

I pray that your heart will be open to giving freely to these very worthy causes. Your donation (large or small) can make a huge difference to the lives of those we are striving to help.

If you wish to contact me for any reason,
my telephone is: + 353 45 529982, e-mail:arthurmc@iol.ie
or to the charity address below:

St. Joseph & The Helpers Charity Ltd
P.O. Box 10486, Dublin 18

DONATIONS

Your donations can be sent in the various ways outlined on the website: www.helperscharity.com or to any of the addresses below:

Ireland
St. Joseph & The Helpers Charity Ltd,
P.O. Box 10486, Dublin 18
Tel: +353 (0) 1 2858130 or +353 (0) 45 529982,
Email: info@helperscharity.
www. helperscharity.com

UK
Pat Henry,
St. Joseph & The Helpers Charity (UK) Ltd,
12 Cangles Close, Boxmoor, Hemel Hempstead,
Herts HP1 1NJ,
England.
Tel, +44 (0) 1442 391087,
Email: info@helperscharity.com
www. helperscharity.com

USA
Sue Pastorini,
Weible Columns, 6814 Larkin Road,
Jacksonville, FL 32211.
USA.
Tel. (904) 726-5004
Email: weiblecolumns@bellsouth.net
www. helperscharity.com

REFERENCES

The New American Bible (Catholic Bible Publishers, Wichita, 1971).

The New Jerusalem Bible Study Edition. (Darton, Longman, Todd, London, 1994).

Catechism of the Catholic Church (Geoffrey Chapman, The Bath Press, London, 1994).

Akers, G. The Stations of the Cross by St. Alphonsus (Redemptorist Publications, Chawton, 1993).

Bauer, J. The Essential Mary Handbook. (Redemptorist Publications, Chawton, 1999).

De Montfort, L. The Secret of the Rosary (Montfort Publications, New York, 1954).

Groeschel, J. The Rosary (Creative Communications, St. Louis, 1995).

McKenna, B. Miracles Do Happen (Veritas Publications, Dublin, 1987).

McKenzie, J. Dictionary of The Bible (Simon & Schuster, London, 1995).

O'Collins, G., Farrugia, E. A Concise Dictionary of Theology, T&T Clark, Edinburgh, 2000).

Wallins, K. A Visit to Lourdes: Spirituality for Today Clemens Production, Bridgeport ,1996).

Woolley, J. I Am With You 2nd. ed., (John Hunt, St. Alresford, 1984).